See It Grow
APPLE

by Dawn Bluemel Oldfield

Consultant: Karen C. Hall, PhD
Applied Ecologist, Botanical Research Institute of Texas
Fort Worth, Texas

BEARPORT
PUBLISHING

New York, New York

Credits

Title Page, © Dhoxax/Shutterstock; TOC, © Alexander Mazukevich/Shutterstock; 4, © Alex Staroseltsev/Shutterstock; 5, © Terrance Emerson/Shutterstock; 6, © images72/Shutterstock; 7, © Vladmir Khodataev/Shutterstock; 8L, © Valentina Razumova/Shutterstock; 8R, © pasmal/amanaimagesRF/Thinkstock; 9, © Valentina Razumova/Shutterstock; 9T, © HorenkO/Shutterstock; 10L, © Fotofermer/Shutterstock; 10R, © Gina Rothfels/Shutterstock; 11, © Jumos/Shutterstock; 12, © konzeptm/Shutterstock; 13, © Dani Vincek/Shutterstock; 14, © WDG Photo/Shutterstock; 15, © AtWaG/iStock; 16, © irin-k/Shutterstock; 17, © FCG/Shutterstock; 18T, © Potapov Alexander/Shutterstock; 18B, © daseaford/Shutterstock; 19, © Ann Louise Hagevi/123RF; 20, © Zoroyan/Shutterstock; 21, © Mamuka Gotsiridze/Shutterstock; 22, © Alexander Mazukevich/Shutterstock; 22T, © Steve Heap/Shutterstock; 22B, © iris wright/Shutterstock; 23 (T to B), © AtWaG/iStock, © Thomas Oswald/Dreamstime, © photosync/Shutterstock, © images72/Shutterstock, © Valentina Razumova/Shutterstock, and © pasmal/amanaimagesRF/Thinkstock; 24, © Dhoxax/Shutterstock.

Publisher: Kenn Goin
Editor: Jessica Rudolph
Creative Director: Spencer Brinker
Design: Debrah Kaiser
Photo Researcher: Olympia Shannon

Library of Congress Cataloging-in-Publication Data

Bluemel Oldfield, Dawn, author.
  Apple / by Dawn Bluemel Oldfield.
     pages cm. — (See it grow)
  Summary: "In this book, readers learn how apples grow from seed to fruit"— Provided by publisher.
  Audience: Ages 3–8.
  Includes bibliographical references and index.
  ISBN 978-1-62724-839-6 (library binding) — ISBN 1-62724-839-0 (library binding)
  1. Apples—Juvenile literature. I. Title. II. Series: See it grow.
  QK495.R78B58 2016
  634.11—dc23
                          2015015274

For more information, write to Bearport Publishing Company, Inc., 45 West 21st Street, Suite 3B, New York, New York 10010. Printed in the United States of America.

10 9 8 7 6 5 4 3

Contents

Apple 4

Apple Facts 22

Glossary 23

Index. 24

Read More 24

Learn More Online. 24

About the Author. 24

Apple

Apples are a delicious fruit.

They are round, crisp, and juicy.

How did they get that way?

Apples can be red, green, pink, or yellow.

Apples grow on trees.

Apple trees start out as tiny seeds.

An apple seed is a little bigger than a grain of rice.

seed

Apple seeds grow in the soil.

First, **roots** form and reach downward.

Then, a green **shoot** grows up out of the ground.

shoot

seed

root

Leaves start to form.

leaf

All plants need water to grow. Their roots take in water from the soil.

Over several months,
the shoot gets taller.

After a few years, the shoot becomes a tree.

The young tree has many branches.

A young apple tree is called a sapling.

Over time, the tree grows taller and taller.

Buds grow on its branches.

bud

Apple trees can grow more than 40 feet (12 m) tall.

13

In spring,
the buds open.

Blossoms grow out of each bud.

Apple blossoms are pink and white.

15

The blossoms have **pollen** that bees use for food.

Bees fly from flower to flower to gather the pollen.

As they fly, they spread the pollen.

By spreading pollen, bees help make new plants.

pollen

Soon, the blossoms fall off.

Tiny fruits start to grow on the branches.

The fruits are apples. Each apple is attached to the tree by a stem.

stem

Over a few months, the apples get bigger.

They change color as they grow.

By fall, the apples are ready to eat.

20

Inside each apple is a **core** that holds tiny seeds.

Some of these seeds might grow into new apple trees!

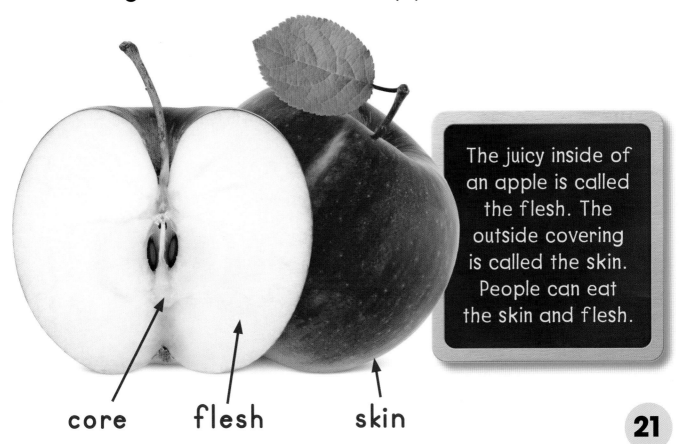

core   flesh   skin

The juicy inside of an apple is called the flesh. The outside covering is called the skin. People can eat the skin and flesh.

Apple Facts

🌸 There are more than 12,500 kinds of apples grown all over the world. They have names like Granny Smith, Red Delicious, and Pink Lady.

🌸 Apples are used to make pies, sauces, juices, and many other foods and drinks.

🌸 Some apples are a little larger than a cherry. Others are as big as a grapefruit.

🌸 An apple tree can live for more than 100 years.

Glossary

 **blossoms** (BLOSS-uhmz) flowers on a fruit tree or other plant

 **buds** (BUDZ) small growths on the branches of plants that turn into leaves and flowers

 **core** (KORE) the tough center of an apple where the seeds are found

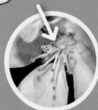 **pollen** (POL-in) tiny yellow grains made by flowering plants; plants use pollen to help make new plants

 **roots** (ROOTS) parts of a plant that take in water and food from the soil

 **shoot** (SHOOT) a young plant that has just appeared above the soil

Index

bees 16–17

blossoms 15, 16–17, 18

buds 13, 14–15

fruit 4, 18

roots 8–9, 10

seeds 7, 8, 21

shoot 8, 10

soil 8–9

tree 6, 11, 12–13, 18, 21, 22

Read More

Esbaum, Jill. *Apples for Everyone (Picture the Seasons).* Washington, DC: National Geographic (2009).

Harris, Calvin. *Apple Harvest (All about Fall).* Mankato, MN: Capstone (2008).

Learn More Online

To learn more about apples, visit
www.bearportpublishing.com/SeeItGrow

About the Author

Dawn Bluemel Oldfield is a writer. She enjoys reading, traveling, and working in her garden. She and her husband live in Prosper, Texas.